Bending into the Light

ALICE ATTIE

Bending into the Light

LONDON NEW YORK CALCUTTA

Seagull Books, 2023

Text and images © Alice Attie, 2023

ISBN   978 1 8030 9 168 6

British Library Cataloguing-in-Publication Data
A catalogue record for this book is available from the British Library

Typeset by Seagull Books, Calcutta, India
Printed and bound by Hyam Enterprises, Calcutta, India

for
Muriel

To write: to try meticulously to retain something, to cause something to survive; to wrest a few precise scraps from the void as it grows, to leave somewhere a furrow, a trace, a mark or a few signs.

Georges Perec

One about a man, another about a woman, a third about a thing and finally one about an animal, a bird probably.

Samuel Beckett

When She Died, the Tipping Began

The trees to one side fell.

The sea against the surf heaved

sigh

after

sigh

In the middle of the night

stars into darkness dropped.

The far and the near flooded the gates.

The mind, now scorched,

begins again.

What

disturbs the branch

is

what you wanted to say

is

where the poem begins

Ten Selves

The first one was a sayer   he said all things that came to him   all things that the mind could

all things that the mouth could   all things

The second one was a saver   she saved all things to keep   all things tiny   all things grand

she saved and kept all things

The third one was a looker   all things he gazed upon   all things he considered   all things
he held

up to the light   to turn and turn and look upon   all things

The forth one wasn't able   she was unsure in all things   she wavered   in all things
her mind travelled back

and travelled forth   in all things she was uncertain

The fifth one was a counter   he counted the days   he counted the steps taken   he
counted things

heaped in piles   counted all things in view   he counted them

The sixth one was outside   from all things   she stood outside   towards all things she
swerved

from all things was distant   from the centre and from the sides   from all things she
stood afar

The seventh one repeated   all things he heard he repeated   all things he read he read again

all things he passed   he turned to pass again   all things he imagined again and again and again

The eighth one was in the middle of   always in the middle of   the stirrings   she was in the middle

of the crowd   in the middle of   the commotion   in the middle of   surrounded by all

The nineth one wrote it down   he heard and wrote down what he heard   he dreamt and wrote

what he dreamt   he wrote down all things known   all things imagined

The tenth on was an embellisher   she heard the stories and expanded them   she thought and

her thoughts grew   she adorned all things   all things she enhanced

Such That

A line circles and circumvents
loosening the perimeter

the way a gust of wind
is suddenly upon us

breaking up breaking down
dropping its purpose

rounding our hearts
tracing our fear

loosening the perimeter
to become part of

the poverty of everything
loosening the perimeter

circling and circumventing
dropping its purpose

resting in the unrest
where loneliness is a victory

The Cruellest Month

listen

dark is speaking dark

thought is speaking thought

imagination is speaking imagination

listen

I heard it once

I heard it twice

cloud speaking cloud

listen

the mountain is speaking mountain

shape is speaking shape

heart is speaking heart

listen

someone somewhere is speaking

there and there and there

grief is speaking grief

Names

catch fire
cut through the air

opening our mouths
pecking at our tongues

one by one
we *swallow*

we *warbler*
we *finch*

mourning dove
tanager

nibbling at the ear
whip-poor-will

yellowthroat
humming

one by one
listening for names

Waiting

When the pond is shallow
you can see small fish

hovering beneath the surface
and sometimes

in a rhythm

unlike anything
they dash

in a rhythm

from not having
to having

sometimes
you see them

sometimes
you don't

in a rhythm

sometimes
when the pond is shallow.

Reading George Oppen

lines around which I pause

> *Obsessed, bewildered*
> *By the shipwreck*
> *Of the singular*
>
> *We have chosen the meaning*
> *Of being numerous.*

comprehension

> *Most simple*
> *Most difficult*

irretrievable

> *whether, as the intensity of seeing increases, one's distance*
> *from them, the people, does not also increase*
> *I know, of course, I know, I can enter no other place*
>
> *Yet I am one of those who from nothing but a man's way of*
> *thought and one of his dialects and what has happened*
> *to me*
> *Have made poetry*

because I am

> *Unable to begin.*

The Sublime

pitches us into blackness

a far field

a far city

a far speech

is

what we fear

is

by another name

beauty

the night
is
a blue
mis-
under-
standing
trill-
ing the vowell-
ed bird
into
the
mut-
able
into
long-
ing
into
mouth-
ing
a blue
night
blu-
ing
into
obliv-
ion

Migrations

all night I heard the breath of darkness

all night the unknowing of speech

all night strange birds howling

all night memories

all night their fierce orbits wobbling

all night groaning

all night overtaking

all night migrating

all night heaving into odds and evens

all night pulled into the light

all night the hollowing

all night everywhere

all night turning to you

all night

Stay

I can carry you.

Stay

I can sing to you.

Stay

I can rock you.

Stay

Why

because love is nothing if it bends when bending

because our desires alight in darkness

because knowledge swerves

because in the mind there is a semblance

because the pen strays

because shapes come into view

because if I die before I wake

My Father Under the Oak Tree

My father roots in the soil of the oak.
His soft voice below the land seeps
its sweet harmonies to the roots.

I study the leaves.
I study the veins
how they fall about the central stem in fine filigree.

The veins of my hands and the veins of the leaves
are rivers running from here to there
into the soil, into the oak roots.

The whistle of winds
the din of swaying branches
tune their hallelujahs to the soil's pulse.

A swarm of ladybugs
lifts, spreading red wings
into a flurry of confusion.

The sky resonates with whites and blues.
Blood juices through the foliage.
Leaves descend, balletic.

Sweet harmonies seep into the roots.

Rustling

When the screen door closes

when birds inch their way across the sky

when the edge of the mountain shimmers before darkness takes it

you hear them.

In flashes of recognition,

you imagine them.

Expelled from their devotions,

their uncertain selves are rocking.

In flashes of recognition,

you imagine them

ephemeral for the eye, suspended

for the mind, swarming for the ear.

You imagine them, again and again.

Mass in B Minor

When the sirens traverse the city, we are reminded.

The uppermost book on the pile is a small volume that Artur sent from Warsaw, *The History of Disappearance*.

The tulips are shrivelling.

Everything is in memory of.

When I sat down to read the opening passage, I remembered, not the passage itself, but the train ride from Paris to Zurich, the landscape escaping at such speed, the way the book garnered meaning, profoundly.

As one ages, one understands the unbecoming of becoming.

The first notes ride tremulously into the blue air.

The telescope could, in theory, detect, from here on earth, the heat of a bumble-bee flapping its wings on the moon.

Each its own aura, its own being, its own disappearance.

She is in conversation with another whom she cannot name. The disturbances of longing impel her. She sees herself everywhere. In the margins of the night, she composes a catalogue of desire. She would like this to be a topic, to have no object, to desist in its own addresses. She imagines a figure scrawled for the eye, traced for the hand. Her dreams travel in darkness, and in darkness they dissolve.

She appears to others as the one she imagines herself to be. She finds no metaphor for this. To anchor her thoughts, she takes hold of the shapes that populate her mind. As she opens and closes her eyes, words accumulate. They are stitched and unstitched. They converge in a quilting of desire. Her longing rests in language. Its edges are blunted by the axe of silence. The ruddy contours of the heart push against her. She dreams.

Flesh to flesh, words touch. They tumble through the mind. She questions their excesses. Her thoughts begin to transfigure. They are ribbons wrapping, folding and unfolding into large ineffable events. She casts about the room. When her eyes open, they rest on the surface of things. Thoughts become scandalous, flinging their flames into darkness. Everywhere, she senses complicity.

There are stories she wishes to tell. Words fall like chips from the avalanche of

language. They hang, small and indecipherable. In the middle of the night,

a million lights to light her way. Desire enters and leaves through an invisible

door. The air is drenched, dropping its hot breath. Moonlight begins and ends.

Small sounds rise and fall. She converses with another whom she cannot name.

Majestic

the way the sun pours light on the heads of flowers

the way we coax words, shuffling and dealing them

the way we are hoisted into time

to be thrown back

to go round and round

the way

I miss you more now that you are next to me

now that we are tipping into infinities

There is a poem in the heavy hang of clouds
in the tree bark

in the child tumbling
in the reader reading

There is a poem in the calculation of a distant galaxy
in years of light distancing

in the lamp's arc
in desire desiring

There is a poem in the note diminishing
in last looks

in the song
in the unseen

There is a poem in the man walking
in the woman shuffling

in the conflux of voices
in the saxophone sounding

There is a poem in the train approaching
in longing

in mourning
in the sky dimming

There is a poem
in the heart's red fire

Bending

Something bends inside her. Something down in the belly is bending.

Ideas bend the mind. She carries them. One by one, they bend,

crack and furrow. She bends into one. She bends into another.

When there are no more, there will be no more bending.

Being

I open and close my hands. My hands are bellows. They open and close.

I spread my fingers. They are webbed where they meet the palms.

I am fisted when I close my hands and fanned when I open them.

I push my palms forward. I bend my wrists.

I swing my arms.

I swing them from side to side, from side to side.

When stones fill our pockets, we slow down.

She
is
by the shore
culling
and
the
birds
are
bickering
and
the
water
lapping
and
the
light
swelling
and
her
thoughts
sorrowing
and
the
gull
gutting
into
the
blue
sea
into
the
blue
sky
tossing

Haecceity

Too much as they are to be changed by metaphor.
—Wallace Stevens

The body at noon, shadowless, in sun's exactitude, unwavering, measures itself.

Light moves, morphing form into un-form, a calligraphy writing the hour.

Invisible hands, as if touching, as if rubbing, seduce what will be from what is.

All is fugitive along the surface.

Strangers in view, cleave and breach.

Once they pass by, they are no more.

The one who sings aloud and the one whose head is bowed.

A child climbing the wooden beam.

Being in immanence, without remainder.

The crease along the sky begins to shake loose.

Permutations of suchness, lingering.

Luminous

I was a solid among solids.
—Samuel Beckett

Contiguous with the boundary of one is the boundary of another.

The inscrutable is and will be. What constitutes being is this thing,

A metaphysical casting its shadow, putative and indubitable.

Thinking catachrestic: Say one thing when the other means.

Thinking sublimity: Inimitable is the day drifting.

Diurnal is the setting of the sun, tensile against the sky.

From this vantage point, everything. The ear into all, leans.

Elsewhere, consubstantial with appearance, illusions,

Pronounced as the selves of ourselves, gather.

Solids are posturing. Indemonstrable and innominate.

To the eye, they are unbidden. For the mind, they are posited,

Poised in perfection. As things among things, they are.

A murmur of birds

swerves

into

V

into

S

Vanishing

what the sea

what the sky

what the trees

tell us

The Leaves of the Aspen

Quiver

at night, they chorus in small crescendos.

Our lives are stitched

Into years, months, days, hours.

There are echoes doubling the world,

bouncing across the field.

I am loosened from my moorings.

I am set wandering.

Fluencies

The sun inches closer, throwing shadows.

Soon, it will be time.

Mystery like a nomad will roam the hills.

Soon, illusions, like seeds, will scatter.

The real will overtake us

Pitching these sounds into grammar.

A voice, high-pitched, will pierce the silence, sorrowful, ruminative.

I will feel the ground trembling.

Mystery like a nomad will roam the hills.

She will gather her stray hairs and tuck them behind her ears

Whispering

Here is a feather for your pain

Remember

she

once

in

love

was

and

love

was

once

all

in

love

she

once

was

and

all

was

once

love

come dear one   come
steady the undone doings
steady the divisions divided
steady time in the branch visible

come dear one   come
be close   be near from far
as time in increments of time
suspends

come   wander with me
come
listen to the rain
its radiance   its rhythm

tapping the mind
as the chirp of a bird
I thought I saw   I thought I heard
will be for us   something

ineffable
as the hawk circling
as we walk the long loop
along the long afternoon

the frogs   in small clusters
dropping their croaks into silence
leaning into reeds
their gold tones   in chords

heaving us into thought
come dear one   come
be close   be near from far
be steady as the tree is steady

as the bird seeing your eye
seeing
is a mystery
tumbling through us

measuring the hours   the days   the years
as we are   as we were   as we will be
in time   present
in silence   present

here   and here   and here
is tumbling through us
steadying the stranger knocking at the door
steadying the voice breaking up   breaking down

steadying the oak
whose branches swing
whose leaves flutter
come   steady us

as word to page
come into the reach of language
come into the moment
come

as the sun against the cloud
just barely in slow season   comes
just barely as darkness into daylight
comes   be close   be near from far

Evening Comes

The finch extends her pouch to let the dove peck.

She twists and pulses her head.

She bows to the dove's beak poking.

The big-bellied bird is perplexed.

Soon it will be time for bed.

The lights will dim.

The fish in their tanks will float

into oblivion, into the darkened blue.

I will tuck you in.

I will tip-toe out.

The subjunctive mood

is

ought

is

as if

because the possible

could be

There

was a time
was what was

was something
was unlike anything

was glistening in the white light
was enough to touch

was enough to hear
was enough to see

was unlike anything
was all

Searching

the sound of the trumpet in the distance

the moon barely in focus

the hiker along the ridge

the screech of a car

the tangle of thinking

my mother-tongue searching

Study in Black and White

I am thinking in a dark room
with my skirt just so
with my arms hugging my legs
with my hands clasped
with my heart unknowing
with my face in shadow
with my knees draped over the chair
I am drawn into it, into something.

Where are you now that you are no more?

Nothing to Speak Of

but the slow bird circling

but the translucence

but small objects left to their small selves

but the difference between them

but the elegance of hands moving

but the pulse of the heart

but presence

Intuition

midnight
black grasses teaming
instinct and urgency

glowing
bursts of desire
syncopate

skimming the surface
finding
letting go

multitudes
beckoning
birthing into alphabets

Sunday Afternoon in the Park

Birds. Bicycles. Runners. In the distance. Sirens.

Conversations close. Conversations far. On the pavement. Hexagons.

Patterns. A man in a wide-brimmed hat. Another by his side.

Stepping in tandem. Side by side. Coupling. Two by two. A dog leaps. Settles.

Two by two. In celebration. Little girl in pink tutu. Celebration.

Bus stops. Doors swing open. On and off. Engine revving. Looking.

Thinking. Where we go. What we see. Time. Long after I am. Trees.

Spring. Will be. Still. Will be. Looking. A woman by the garbage. Sifts.

Gleans. What to think. To look. Not to look. Another. In flowered dress. Colours.

Patterns. A child in a stroller. Whimpering. Feet touching. Swaying. Trees.

Squirrel. Poised. Branch. Swaying. Bounds. Dog. Fetches. Runs. Fetches.

Runs. Drops. Looks. Thinks. Pink. Yellow. Sun. Squinting. Look. Don't look. Here.

What we see. There. Blue balloon. Rising. Sun. Yellow. Don't look. Look. Ball dropping.

Sun falling. Doors closing. All is. In the eye of the beholder. Down by the Riverside.

I love the rain
drumming

the tree
budding

its shadow
dancing

the river
flowing

the wind
winnowing

the feather
fumbling

I love
the wilting roses

worlds hidden
worlds revealed

I love
what we know

what we will never know
the half

that is ours and
the half that never will be

Doubling

I saw him from the corner of my eye

his curls were golden

as he turned to look

the light pronounced him

how he stood

how he watched

how when we turned

to go, the light threaded

patterns along the horizon

the air drew its airy breath

and we fell, one by one

into the arms of memory

Into the crooked world
the crooked mind wanders.
A young man is reading on a bench under a tree.
The crooked tree is leaning into him,
leaning into his story.
Bells are ringing the hour.
Midday, the purple air is pulsing.
The branches are chipped,
revealing patterns, peeling
in swirls, to be drawn
in and out of
clarity and confusion.
The bells chime in certainty.
All around, a vying for attention.
Inching my way forward,
I throw my glance,
catching something, the infinitesimal.
There is nothing to speak of
but the chimes of solace
or the details we cannot see
or clouds blowing across buildings
or colours to consider, blues and greys
transfiguring the sky
sequencing everything
tree, cloud, young man reading
water towers
to count to note
sequencing.

Because not to think of them
is to be inside them.
Because everything elsewhere
is vying for attention.
Because this is all
and this is nothing.
It just is.

see how the pink buds are budding pink

see how everything green is green

see how the grey-blue sky is grey-blue

see how near we are to the colour of being

Enchanting

> This is only here. This is only now.
> —Virginia Woolf

The hills rise, mute in a mute magnificence.

Across the field, the awkwardness of thought.

Water pulls the trees upside down, pooling them among the clouds.

They quiver on the water's skin.

The flowers are standing on wobbly legs.

A bird, sounding like an old swing, sets a branch rocking.

One Among Many

What is it?   What makes it so, the sudden uplift of thought, the repetitions?
Why death, heavy in the heavy step.

I will go into the garden and pick a flower, fold it into a card,
place it in an envelope.

There are two. I can see them. They walk the road near the house.
The air carries their voices. Dim and distinct. One voice above another climbs.

She was so beautiful.
(I didn't know her then.)
Everyone spoke of her beauty.
(Suffering the pains she suffered.)

Phrases, fragmented, ride the wind.
Beyond the trees, the edge of the mountain curves.

She was so beautiful.
(Suffering the pains she suffered.)

We thought about it.
The crows, in black iridescence, cascading into the deep-yellow air.

A certain hour is the colour of naked wood

A certain shadow is the shape of love

A certain song is the future of solitude

This hour is the colour of naked wood

This shadow is the shape of love

This song is the future of solitude

This is the colour of naked wood

This is the shape of love

This is the future of solitude

The colour of naked wood

The shape of love

The future of solitude

The colour

The shape

The future

Wood

Love

Solitude

Schubert in the Library

She is listening to Shubert's C Major Quintet and arranging books on the library table.

She thinks about Schubert

>   how the composer carried Beethoven's casket in the procession

>   how months later, dying in his small bedroom, he longed to hear Beethoven

>   how all things come to an end

The trees are tossing their leaves in the sun.

They toss their branches onto the table, dancing across the books.

She straightens her *back* against the *back* of the chair

thinking about *shapes*, about words: her *back* against the *back* of the chair

>   how books lift their *shapes* among the branches

Shape is a word that *shapes*

She remembers by the sea

>   how the stones were round   *shaped* by time

>   giggling in the surf   ancient   they moved silver in the silver light.

In the library, she listens.

Schubert, she thinks, is *shaping* my sadness.

She watches the light of the sun

      how the sea glistened

      how from the surf   the stones rushed towards her

She straightens her *back* against the *back* of the chair.

The shadows branching on her books slowly disappear.

Proximities

He is restless, laying on his side on a warm afternoon, a cigarette in hand.

Tie askew. He is ill-fitting.

Memory glides over the landscape.

Within it, he is.

The trees blush from having too much.

Their arms are outstretched, reaching.

It is late.

Midday. Midlife. Mid.

Our minds have gone the distance. The length and width of thought.

> *People move towards me.*
>
> *They carry their choices on their backs, stopping to consider.*
>
> *Put your hand on my shoulder.*
>
> *Outstretch me.*

Be sure to check the fireplace.

Be sure.

What time did you say it was?

I didn't say.

I thought I heard a ticking.

the congruous
is
slipping
into
the incongruous
into
concepts
slipping
into
what
is
into
what
is not
into
aporias
into
something
somewhere
vibrat-
ing
into
twilight
fading

Dreaming in Mexico

At night, from under your pillow, a selection of dreams.

You reach for the one from where your father is speaking from the desert town of
La Piedra of the Dirt Gatherers.

The rocks are barren. The hills are barren.

The russet secrets of birds shake the branches.

You dream of pyramids rising out of dust, of steep steps, of a hidden ancient knowledge

Of twilight's crimson glow.

Rogier van der Weyden

Deposition

Christt

is

swooning

his hips

swaying

into her blue

fully

falling

red ribbons

waving

drop

by

drop

pooling

everything

into

the eye

plunging

The Old Man and His Grandson

In the 1480 portrait by Domenico Ghirlandaio,

The red cape of the old man and the red cap of his grandson
absorb the two figures in rapt attention.

The old man thinks about his grandson, about the world before him,
about things that cannot be spoken.

The boy's hand rests on the man's cape. His eyes are uncertain.
He is bewildered by the contours of the old man's face.

The man meditates on the idea of proportion,
on the vanity imbedded in the boy's inquisitive eyes.

The man's nose captivates the young boy
who gazes in wonder at this grandfather's face.

In the distance, a massive rock protrudes form the hillside.
Small shrubs and poplars adorn the green hills.

The world is knobbed and bumped by bushes and trees.
The little boy, enamoured by his grandfather's face,

appears soothed. The landscape becomes one
of outcrop, of meditation and love.

After Wallace Stevens

When Gould stooped over the piano,
his back curved over his shortened chair,
he hovered close, his hands lifting.

As he rummaged among the keys, moaning,
his knees pushed against his face.
He hovered close, his hands lifting.

He rummaged among the keys, moaning,
humming

> *I am*
>
> *I am*
>
> *I am*

Study in Seven Parts

There was the sound of a plucked cello string
    tucked into the pocket of my coat
        was a leaf yellowing

But I envied the philosopher's mind
    how the curtain shivered, just slightly
        how stories are pinched and brief

How desiring bones desire, incandescent,
    coupling and splitting against the dark
        how death overtakes the mind

How the cafe awning shadows a hand writing
    how the central self is centred
        in loneliness, proportioned

How words up and down, side to side
    are figures in the distances approaching
        each a declaration, each persisting

How the counter-tenor sings the Stabat Mater
    the voice has no centre
        for the seeing for the sightless

It rises as the tipping begins

    where being into nothingness spills

       without meaning, over all.

New York City

Along the avenue, pedestrians.

One by one, I count them.

A large dog is pulling his master.

A woman waits for the light to change.

Another on the phone advances.

One by one, I count them.

The Photograph

A man walks down the street of the city. He walks rapidly.

There is a sense of urgency. Behind him, others walk with equal determination.

There is something they know, something they dread.

Knowledge clings. It pushes them, urging them on.

It is winter in Paris. The pavements are covered with snow.

The swoosh of feet in rapid succession, a kind of marching.

The man walks with a wide gait. His eyes fall, uncertain, onto the pavement.

His tie is tucked into his shirt. His belt is cinched, tightly.

The white of his tie, the white of his buckle, the white of the snow.

With his hands in his pockets, he pulls his thoughts closer.

Footfalls. White streets. White snow. A man walking.

Someone has taken this photograph.

An arm swings into the frame.

The cuff of the sleeve suggests a woman. Her gait is swift.

There is another, a man walking behind, his pants wide, his white socks pronounced.

His dark hair is pulled back from the high forehead.

They are fleeing. Time is running out.

Someone turns around, seizes the moment.

Silence but for the rhythm of footsteps, of arms swinging.

Someone has taken this photograph.

White tie, white socks. white snow, the cuff of her coat.

Time is running out.

If You Follow the 8

If you play it this way

if you set the curve in motion

if the position is right

the probability

increases

in a series of arabesques

to the right

or

to the left

a ball

will

drop into

a pocket

to score

if you play it right

if you set the curve in motion

Unutterable

my undone self is unfurling
unburdened unguarded and unnameable
unfollowing the undulant un-paths of the unsayable
my undoing is uninked its unmeaning ungloved
in ungenerous times the unthinking is unseen
it unveils the unfettered to unhear

to unhear the unheard the unopposed
the hour unsounding into itself is unfolding
unmasked unvoiced unread and unwritten
our uncommon unselves are unimagined
unbending into the unbidden is the unsaid
unthinking and unending

Words appear strange as he writes them.

They arrive fully formed, drifting onto the page.

When ideas come, they come suddenly. He catches them midair, choosing.

He sits at the table, funnelling his thoughts, moving his hand,

The lines are curling, folding, whirling into language.

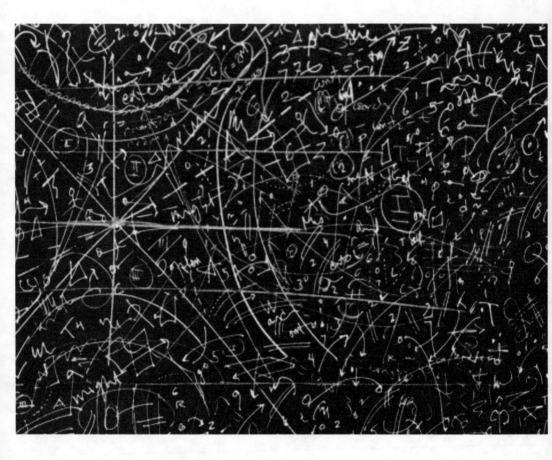

Disquiet

The mind

in arcs of deliberation

divides

the fractured

from the whole

portioning

the finite

from the infinite

mapping

latitudes

slipping into

longitudes

singles into

plurals

neutrals into

colours

here

bruising earth

there

fending off silence

Somewhere

Their pink daughters are crossing into the pink elsewhere.

Everywhere pink walls tumbling pink into the pink night.

The children climb the pink hills of their pink imaginations.

Animals scurry in pink confusion.

Pink dreams and pink nightmares into pink flames bursting.

Dedication

And in a far land, bombs are falling.

And the violin is like a cry and when silence comes, you hear it still.
If you move closer, you hear hearts throbbing.
If you step back, the slow cloud grows red.

There are things. This one a toy. This one a namesake. To keep.
A photograph. An old woman weeping. A young woman weeping.
They fill the world with weeping.

Something into something disappears.
And the violin is like a cry.
And the dark day is darkening. Smouldering.

If you were by my side, we would hear them, their strained arias.
If you were near me, we would hear their long laments.
Into forever, we would hear them, falling.

Incomparable

From the book, a phrase: *all pains are incomparable*.

The imagination stirs. *Incomparable*. Into the unimaginable.

The trees are what they are. Standing for something. *Incomparable*.

Flower petals open and close. They will fall and fade.

The rain will fall. Under the awning, a woman will fall.

Another will pass. Sorrows against the sun, will fall.

Autumn is in the reach of colour. From the trees, leaves will fall.

We cast our eyes on the world. From the general, we choose the particular.

The smallest signifies. It cannot be otherwise. Time, into each, will fall.

Our bodies will end.

All the pages will be written.

Some Sources
and Acknowledgements

PAGE 3 | Georges Perec, *Species of Spaces and Other Pieces* (John Sturrock trans.). London: Penguin, 1997, p. 92.

Samuel Beckett, 'Malone Dies' in *Molloy, Malone Dies, The Unnamable: A Trilogy*. New York: Alfred A. Knopf-Everyman's Library, 1997, p. 205.

PAGE 14 | George Oppen, *New Collected Poems* (Michael Davidson ed.). New York: New Directions, 2002 , pp. 163–88.

PAGE 70 | A photograph found at Clignancourt Market, Paris, 2003.

PAGES 72, 74, 76 | White markings by Alice Attie on the photographs of her late father, Joseph Attie.

PAGE 78 | Photograph of black board with white ink by Alice Attie, New York, 2012.

●

I dedicate these poems to my mother, Muriel, who passed away from Covid in 2020. She remains a life force that presses through me.

I thank my precious children, Justine and Gideon.

I thank my dear love, Royce.

Love has no bounds.

I nod to Georges Perec, George Oppen, Virginia Woolf, Samuel Beckett, Wallace Stevens, Roland Barthes, and to Jorge Luis Borges, whose compass always pointed towards the infinite.

Gratitude to the incomparable team at Seagull Books.

To Naveen Kishore, poet, photographer, an inspiration and dear friend.